THE
LION KING

The cub's parents named him Simba.

"Remember that I will always be there to guide you."
"I will remember," said Simba.

Simba, the playful cub, would reign over
his father's kingdom someday.

Simba met another cub.
Her name was Nala.

Scar wanted to be rid of Mufasa and Simba.
He had hyenas do his spying and trickery for him.

Simba slept, and when he finally woke up,
a meerkat named Timon was staring at him.

© Disney

TIMON

The meerkat became Simba's friend.

PUMBAA

And so did a warthog!

"*Hakuna matata*—no worries!
That's how we live!"

"That's right! No worries!" said Simba.

No responsibilities...

...just carefree living all day.

Simba was thrilled to see Nala again.

King Simba and Queen Nala had a daughter.

The Circle of Life continued.

One morning, there was great excitement in the forest.
Friend Owl was spreading the news.

Owl told everyone about a new prince
who had just been born.

The young prince was a fawn named Bambi,
the son of a noble stag, the Great Prince of the Forest.

© Disney

"Welcome, young prince!" hooted Friend Owl.
Bambi was just waking up by his mother's side.

"Hello, Bambi," the animals and birds added in chorus.

"Yes, good morning!" cried another voice from above.
It was a mother opossum and her three babies.

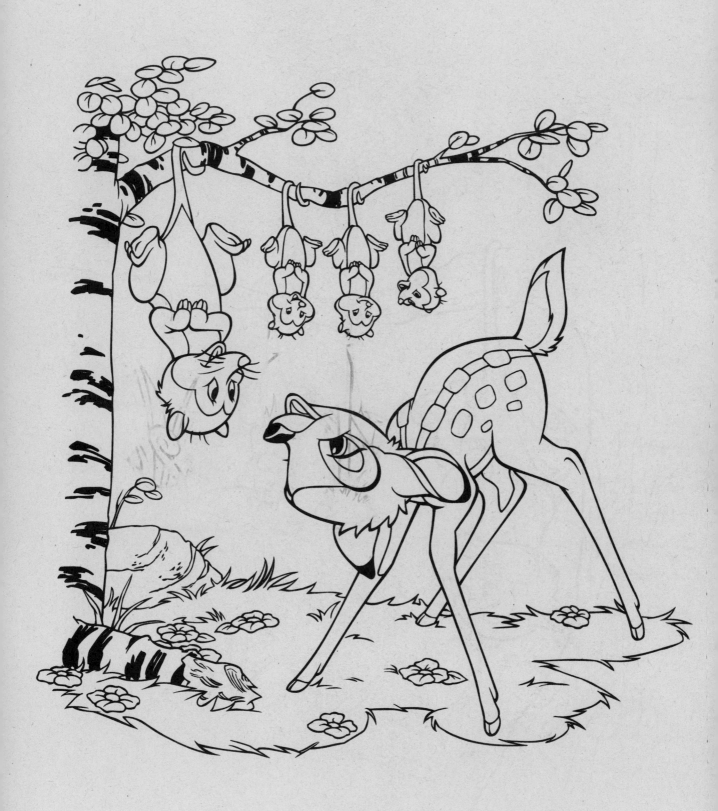

"The forest is a wonderful place!" thought Bambi,
as he looked at the opossums hanging by their tails.

And Mother Quail had eight babies!

"Hiya, Bambi," said a little gray rabbit.

"I'm thumpin'! That's why they call me Thumper!"

"Whatcha wanna do now?" Thumper asked.

"Come on—I'll show you around!"

Bambi and Thumper became best friends.

One Christmas, Jim Dear gave Darling a cuddly present.

© Disney

"Why, she's a perfectly beautiful little *Lady*!" cried Darling.

Jim Dear and Darling petted and pampered Lady.

She loved watching over the house, bringing
Jim Dear his paper, and playing in the yard.

When she was six months old, Lady got a new collar.

A Scottie named Jock became Lady's good friend.

Trusty, a bloodhound, was her friend and neighbor, too.

A friendly mutt named Tramp
didn't live in Lady's neighborhood.

A gang of street dogs chased Lady,
but Tramp rescued her.

Tramp took Lady to his favorite place for dinner.

Tony and Joe serenaded the happy couple.

Lady and the Tramp had a delicious spaghetti dinner.

Tramp traded in his free-wheeling days
for a home with Lady.

Soon, Lady had her own puppies.

They are a family.

Lady and Tramp will love each other forever.

With Jim Dear and Darling,
they all lived together as a family.

101 DALMATIANS

Roger Radcliffe was a musician who lived
in London with his Dalmatian dog, Pongo.

Pongo gazed out the window
while Roger made up songs on the piano.

He saw a little Pekinese riding in the basket of a bicycle...

...and a fancy poodle prancing down the street.

Wait! There was a lady and her beautiful Dalmatian!

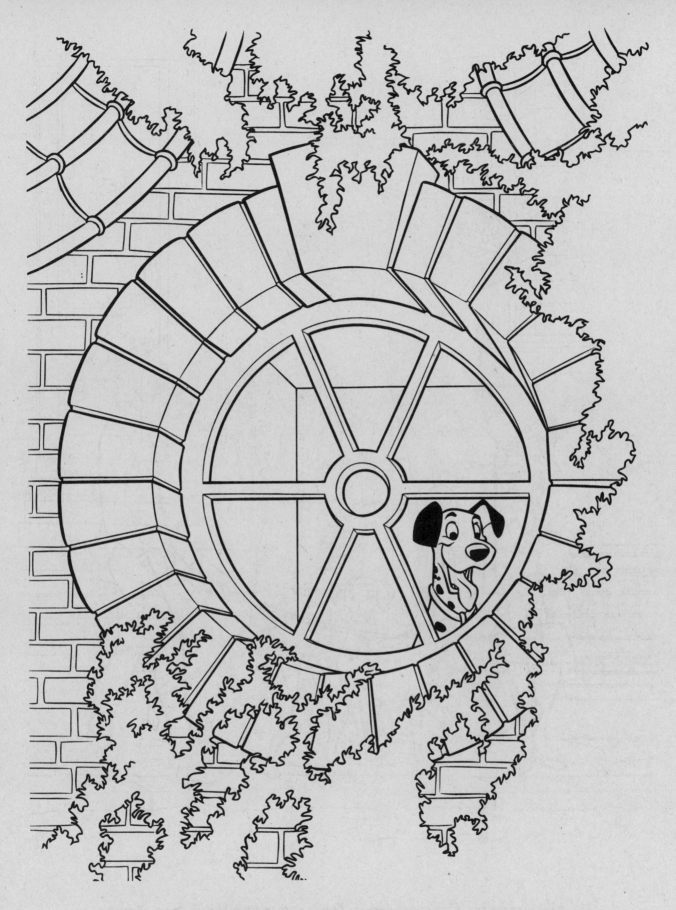

"They're headed for the park," thought Pongo.

In the park, Roger and Pongo strolled by Anita
and her sweet Dalmatian, Perdita.

It was fun to snatch Roger's hat!

Pongo tangled his leash around Roger and Anita.

Roger married Anita,
and Pongo wed Perdita.

© Disney

Pongo found out he was going to be a father!
Perdita was having puppies!

"The puppies are here!" said Nanny.
"And there are 15 of them!"

The puppies liked to crowd around the television set
before being tucked into bed.

The puppies liked to watch Westerns,
with galloping horses.

© Disney

Roger and Anita decided to keep all the puppies
and have a Dalmatian plantation!

Candid Puppy Shots

© Disney

"Congratulations!" the stork said,
setting a baby elephant down in Mrs. Jumbo's train car.

© Disney

Dumbo loved his mother.

"WHOO WHOO! Chugga, Chugga, Chugga!"
Casey Junior, the circus train, raced down the track.

**Mrs. Jumbo gave Dumbo baths,
making sure to wash behind his ears!**

Dumbo loved the tub! He could make fountains
and blow bubbles with his trunk!

Timothy the mouse was Dumbo's best friend.

Timothy thought Dumbo should be in a show.

The little mouse with big ideas
considered elephant pyramids.

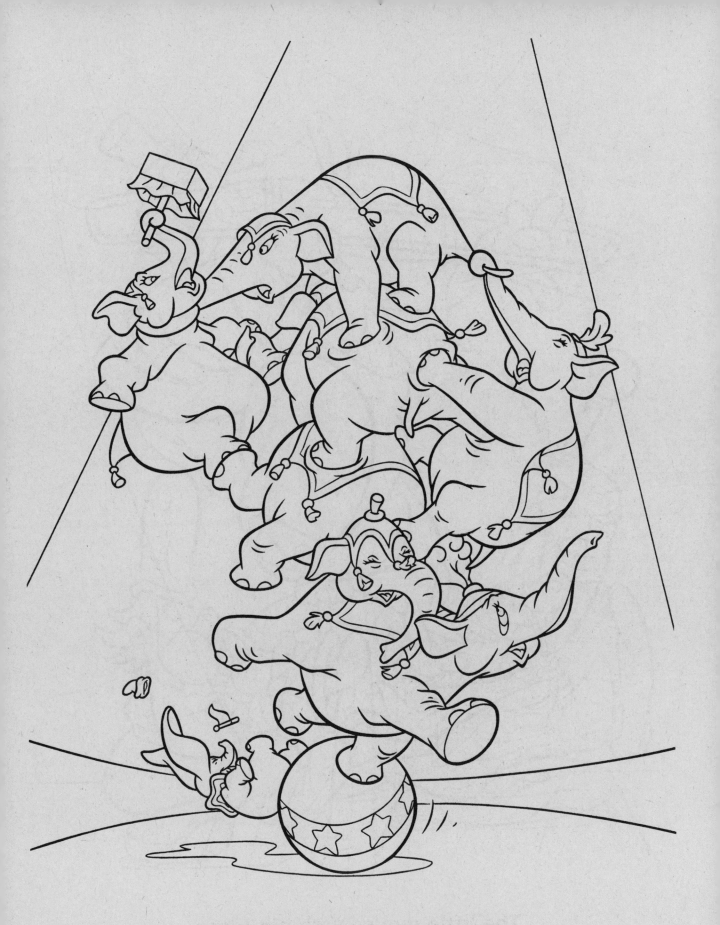

But they were dangerous!

What about a clown act?

He could balance peanuts on his head
and had ideas about making Dumbo famous.

© Disney

Sometimes, Dumbo played hide-and-seek with his mother.

Dumbo, Mrs. Jumbo's baby with the big,
floppy ears, brought up the rear.

He held on to her tail, following her everywhere.

"Dumbo could *really* make people smile!" Timothy thought.

He was the cutest of all the circus babies.

He was fun.

Dumbo could carry a flag...

...or learn to juggle!

Dumbo was spunky.

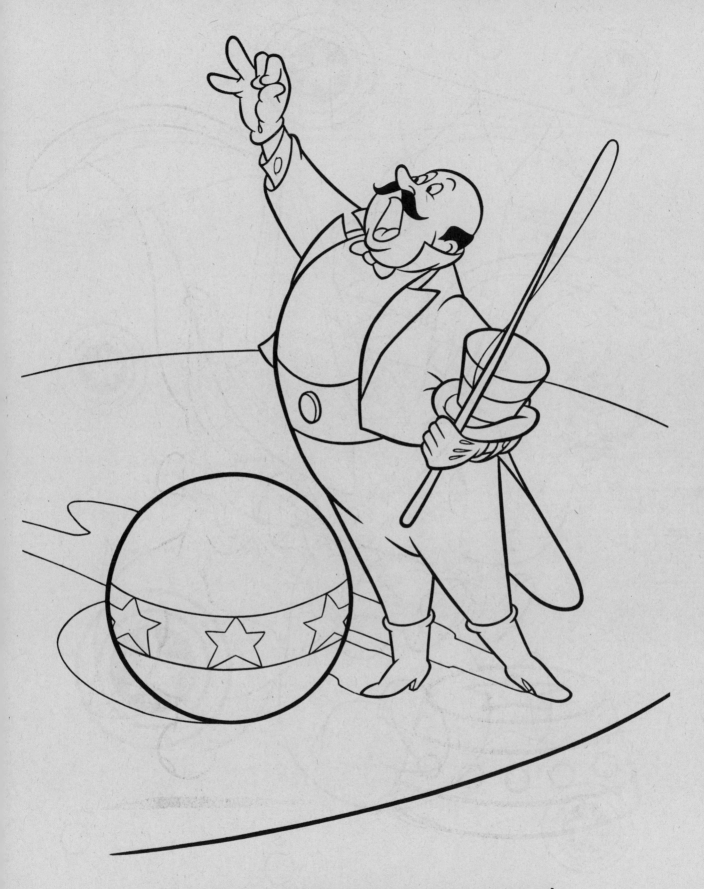

One night, the Ringmaster announced
that Dumbo would be in the act.

Timothy's promise had come true—Dumbo was famous!

"We did it!" Timothy said, as the audience cheered.
"Now you're a star!"

But, best of all, everybody loved Dumbo.

"Dumbo, I just knew you'd be famous someday!"

"I always knew you were special!" said his mother.